I0123091

Shenanigans

Volume I

Public Sector
Personnel Practices
Case Study

Bea Dukes

Dukes Publishing

Shenanigans

Volume I

Public Sector
Personnel Practices
Case Study

Bea Dukes

Shenanigans
Volume I

Public Sector Personnel Practices
Case Study

Copyright@2011 by Bea Dukes
Printed in the United States of America.
www.ShenanigansCaseStudies.com

ISBN-10: 098335491X
ISBN-13: 9780983354918

AUTHOR's NOTE:

This case study is based on an actual real work situation. For privacy reasons, the names have been changed. While we have made every effort to provide accurate information in this book, it is possible that omissions and/or errors may have been inadvertently introduced. While we have made every effort to provide accurate information in this book, it is possible that omissions and/or errors may have been inadvertently introduced. Because of the dynamic nature of the internet, any web links published in this book, may have changed since publication of this work and may be no longer valid.

Dedication

This book is dedicated to everyone with an interest in studying case studies that involve personnel practices within the public sector.

www.ShenanigansCaseStudies.com

Acknowledgements

I am very grateful for my daily inspirational guidance. A special thanks to everyone that shared their real world experiences. The facts and circumstances surrounding the Shenanigans Case Studies are real.

I am very appreciative for the support of my loving family for untiring efforts. Thanks for sacrificing those moments of family time to help me deliver this project.

Thanks to all of my extended family. You have always been there for me. I am very grateful for my special friends.

To those I mentor and to the youth: your individual successes are pivotal to the collaborative progress of your generation and to the generations that follow. You can make the world a better place to live....one decision at a time....

Behind Closed Doors

Behind Closed Doors

Introduction

Shenanigans Volume I, is a case study in Public Sector Personnel Practices. It examines the morality, legality, and ethical actions involved with management selections, talent management and other actions involved in the recruitment, selection, and staffing of management positions within a large federal organization.

This detailed case study is written to provide real-world scenarios for those who study human capital management, talent management, law, personnel policy, public policy, public administration, organizational management, business ethics and government.

Behind Closed Doors is based on facts and circumstances that took place within a program office of a large federal organization.

Particularly disturbing is the notion that many of these actions were taken specifically to portray an image of fairness and compliance. Of greater significance is the evidence that it appears that some actions were deliberately taken to avoid hiring highly qualified veterans and other candidates that fall within other federally recognized categories of special considerations.

After each chapter, questions are presented to facilitate discussion and to launch group project efforts to further analyze the contents of this case study.

Chapter 1

The New Federal Manager

Before we even delve into the hiring process and this case study, it is important to understand that within the federal government, our ability to create greater efficiencies and the success of reform efforts and cost savings initiatives rests squarely on the shoulders of today's managers.

As we maneuver through the periods of the Baby Boomers' transitions that produce brain drain and the intellectual tsunami, along with the dynamics of competing needs of the multi-generational workplace, it imperative that managers within the Federal government remain totally committed to making the right decisions with full transparency. Decisions that will benefit the greater good. Decisions that will place in management and leadership those highly capable, well-prepared, totally dedicated, and infectiously motivated candidates. Those managers and leaders will effectively lead the organizations through the required reforms, cost savings measures, and other budget cutting endeavors.

The creative leadership of this kind of federal manager will generate the changes needed that avoid organizational redundancy and eliminate duplicative processes. These managers will motivate and challenge staff and personnel while creatively implementing streamlined business processes required to take the Federal Government to the next level with fiscal soundness. The nation can no longer afford to do business as usual.

Chapter 2

Chapter 2

The Federal Hiring Process

The recruitment and hiring model within most federal agencies consists of some form of the following flow:

- Normally the hiring official, within the program office where the vacancy occurs, submits to the Office of Human Capital (OHC) or Human Resources (HR) Office a request to advertise a vacancy. This request is similar to a supply requisition; however, it contains all of the specific information required to generate a vacancy announcement that will be posted on www.USAJOBS.opm.gov.

- *A vacancy may occur as a result of retirement, termination, reassignment and reorganization or even through a newly created opportunity.*

- *Regardless of how the vacancy was created, most program offices are eager to start the clock for the laborious hiring process. The program office is normally guided by the policies and procedures of the agency's human resource office with all actions being in compliance with agency policies, regulations, and statues.*

- *Although many streamlining efforts are underway, in some instances the hiring process can vary from 45 to 150 days depending upon the hiring model and other factors.*

- Upon receipt and subsequent approval of the request, the HC office posts the announcements in a prescribed manner. The announcement usually appears on USAJOBS (www.usajobs.opm.gov).

- The vacancy announcement will consist of many important criteria including:

  - Opening Date
  - Closing Date
  - Job Series
  - Grade
  - Duty Title
  - Duty Description
  - Job Qualification Requirements
  - Supplemental Questions

- When the vacancy announcement closes, the Office of Human Capital (HC) evaluates the applicants' information against the prescribed criteria for the position.

- After careful review and analysis, a list of eligible applicants is sent to the requesting office. This listing is commonly referred to as "the cert." Technically speaking, it is a list of applicants who are deemed eligible for consideration for the vacancy announcement based on information submitted by the applicants. Some refer to this as the best qualified (BQ) list; however, in this case, we will reserve that term for the next phase.

- Upon receipt of the list, the selection official determines if interviews will be held and develops a list of the best qualified candidates. *(The selection/hiring official is often assisted by technical experts or a panel.)*

- The hiring official conducts interviews.

- After the interviews are conducted, the hiring official and/or panel collaborate and basically rack and stack the applicants.

- If the selection official is not part of the interview panel, the panel may make recommendations on the top 3 to 5 candidates.

- If second interviews are held, only those individuals are invited for an interview. However, if the selection official participates as a member of the panel and if second interviews are being omitted, then the selection official will make a selection as to the No. 1 (i.e. most qualified) candidate for the position.

- The hiring official submits this information to HC.

- The Office of Human Capital notifies the most qualified applicant of the agency's tentative offer decision.

- If applicant accepts the offer of employment HC follows organizational protocol to assist the applicant through the administrative processing and security clearance requirements for entry on duty.

- If an applicant rejects the offer of employment, HC immediately notifies the hiring official.

- Depending on the quality of the remaining individuals who made the BQ List, the selection official may determine that secondary offers are an appropriate course of action.

- *Note: The selection official is usually a member of senior management. This individual holds a pivotal role in the federal hiring process.*

MANAGER
OPENING
APPLY
WITHIN

Chapter 3

The Workplace Scenario

After having spent a few years at a well-known federal organization, Kapitski, a General Schedule, (GS-15) senior staff analyst and well-respected, professional became aware of the organization's decision to fill a GS-15 supervisory (management) vacancy within the program office where she was assigned.

This was a Director-level position. The selectee would be responsible for the overall management of a wide variety of federal programs. This director position had at least six direct reports who served as program/project managers.

Based on the position management structure within the program office, several of the project managers held the same grade as the Director.

Upon learning of this information, many staff members wondered about the ultimate selection.

Kapitski began a review of her personal files to ensure that she had her resume updated with the most recent information.

Chapter 4

The Vacancy Announcement

On the opening date, the organization announced the position on USAJOBS (www. USAJOBS.opm.gov) using a duty description that identified the job requirements and the duties to be performed.

After carefully reviewing the announcement, Kapitski believed that she was well qualified for the position given the information presented. She shared the announcement and her resume with a mentor of the senior-executive service who strongly recommended that she apply for the position.

Kapitski meticulously reviewed and updated her resume to ensure that there were no inadvertent inaccuracies. She submitted the resume and all required documentation well in advance of the closing date.

On the closing date of the announcement, HC commenced the detailed review and analysis of comparing the knowledge, skills, and abilities of the applicants to the vacancy announcement criteria. Shortly thereafter, they issued the listing of best qualified individuals.

Upon receipt of this list, the hiring official reviewed the information presented. As soon as the cert was received closed-door meetings began with many program officials. Some of these meetings involved the hiring official and some did not.

****

- **What is your opinion of the hiring process?**
- **What hiring timeline would you develop?**

Chapter 5

The Interviews

Shortly after receipt of the list, the hiring official determined that interviews would be held with the highest qualified candidates.

Interviews were scheduled over a period of approximately five-seven days. The face-to-face structured-behavioral interviews lasted approximately sixty-ninety minutes and consisted of 15-20 structured questions designed to produce responses in the behavioral, technical, and management related proficiency areas.

As always, there were many informal discussions among program managers as they speculated as to who would be announced as the new "Director."

Chapter 5

Almost immediately after the interviews concluded, the hiring official submitted the package to HC requesting that a tentative offer of employment be made ASAP (as soon as possible) to Dan, an outside applicant.

So, it was determined that would be the man!

****

- What is your opinion of the interview process?
- Would you have done this differently?

Chapter 6
The Tentative Offer

The Office of Human Capital presented the tentative offer to Dan telephonically with a follow-up tentative letter offer via electronic mail.

As soon as the tentative offer was made, program officials announced the hiring official's decision to the program office.

Dan was a highly recognized name within the political circles of his current agency. *Note: Dan was not a member of the hiring agency*. However, this particular technical community had an international presence with deep professional and personnel relationships, mentoring alliances, and networking partnerships around the world.

So it was not a surprise to hear that Dan was offered the supervisory/management position. The HR specialist waited for Dan's call to accept the offer of employment. The program office communicated daily with the Office of Human Capital to verify Dan's arrival date.

****

What is your opinion of the program office's actions?

Chapter 7
The Cart Before the Horse

To reiterate, as soon as the tentative offer was made, the program officials announced that Dan would be the new Director.

This information was announced before the selection official had a chance to notify the internal candidates of their non-selection. It is proper protocol to notify the internal candidates before the announcement is made publicly.

So to mitigate the damages to morale, afterwards, the selection official immediately notified all internal candidates. The selection official told Kapitski that although Dan was the No. 1 candidate, she was indeed the No. 2 candidate. So, *in the highly unlikely event that Dan declined,* the position would be offered to her.

As the other internal applicants were also notified that they were not selected for the position, they were also given individual feedback on their interviews.

As they waited, the office conversations began...... they waited, and waited, and waited.....

****

What is your opinion of the hiring process at this phase?

Chapter 8
The Call

Finally Dan called. Given his current position, HR anticipated that he would easily clear the security processing. They actually expected that Dan had already worked out his departure and reporting date by this time. However, his message was totally unexpected.....

To the Office of Human Capital: Thank you for your offer of employment for the GS-15 Director Position in your program office. After careful consideration, I have made a decision not to accept this offer with your agency.

This call was totally unexpected. Wow, what a blow! The resounding "no" could presumably be heard halls away.

- How could he turn us down?

- Perhaps, he only applied in haste?

- Was he presented a counter offer at his agency?

- Had he heard something about the organization that impacted his decision?

- Maybe it was personal, who knows?

- Had he heard about the internal politics and personnel practices of the program office?

- Why had Dan took so long to respond?

Oh no! Now that Dan their man was gone, Kapitski, the internal candidate, a veteran, a consummate professional with all of the requisite knowledge, skills, and abilities would now get the offer as promised.

Actually Dan took so long to respond that while waiting, the selecting official was actually away on a pre-scheduled family vacation out of the country when the declination reached the program office.

****

- **What happened to Dan?**

- **What are the program office's options?**

Chapter 9

Inter-Office Discussions

Although well qualified, the other senior managers did not agree with the hiring official's decision and commitment to make a secondary offer to Kapitski.

By now, a few happy hours had taken place, many closed-door sessions, and after a couple of round of golf, the powers-to-be had decided that they still wanted to bring in an external candidate to manage these critical programs. Some from the outside would obviously bring a fresh set of ideas and clearly understand the programs in greater detail that an internal candidate.

Very soon, everything became very clear. It was rather obvious that they had a strategic plan to train-wreck the notion of a secondary offer so that they could bring in their friend, Bill, to take the Director position.

Although Bill had not applied for the Director vacancy. It was rumored that senior management decided that they would bring Bill in to manage the division,. But since he had not applied, how would that work? Interoffice conversations had it that Bill was non-select for a different supervisory position.

****

- **What actions do you think they took?**
- **Do you think they were successful?**
- **What guidance would you offer the senior manager?**
- **What guidance would you offer to the selecting official?**
- **Is this a shenanigan in the making?**
- **Does this have shenanigan potential?**

Chapter 10

The Secondary Offer

When Kapitski learned of Dan's declination of the offer of employment for the Director position, she was quite concerned. She remained concerned about the overall health of the organization. Most of the program/project managers were self-starters who needed very little guidance;however, this was sure to be a major upset so-to-speak.

She remembered that she was their No. 2 candidate. What those thoughts came the excitement of a chance to make a difference within the organization. She patiently waited and waited for the call from HC. She waited with anticipation day after day, but the call never came.

Kapitski understood the inter-workings of the program office and possessed the knowledge, skills, and abilities required to perform the duties as Director and to succeed in this position. She also had a vision and understood the strategic approach needed to take the program office to the next level of efficiencies and greater effectiveness. In terns of the job announcement, she clearly exceeded all criteria specified in the job announcement.

However, one day, she was suddenly summoned to meet with the senior managers behind closed doors. The meeting went something like this…

"**Just why did you interview for this position……**"

It was as if she was having a second interview.

"I am aware that you were told that you would be considered for this position;...but you see..... I have other plans…"

As the berating monologue continued, Kapitski finally had an opportunity to ask a question**, "Have the agency's needs changed?"**

After a few seconds elapsed, the atmosphere in the room thickened. The response to Kapitski's question came in this form.…**"Well, here's what I am going to do....."**

(He paused. With a look of disdain, he slowly began again......)

"I am going to cancel this position and re-announce it with a new position description."

(As if he were convincing himself along the way.....)

"Yes, I am going to re-write the position description."

And so it was, the Program Official decided to announce the position again. According to policy, HC would not allow the program office to re-advertise the same position with an open list of qualified candidates.

It soon became apparent that senior management used unorthodox bullying tactics to threaten and coerce Kapitski into withdrawing from the competition. Her withdrawal cleared the way for HC to official post a second announcement for the same job.

For a couple of days, Kapitski tossed and turned throughout the night. She lost her appetite and her migraine headaches returned as she repeatedly played the entire scenario over and over in her mind.

Finally using sharp, yet politically sensitive language, Kapitski submitted a letter to the senior program official notifying him that she voluntarily declined further consideration for the position.

****

- **Was the agency in compliance with the legal framework of hiring practices?**

- **Did the organization commit an improper personnel practice?**

- **Did the organization commit itself to an improper personnel practice?**

Chapter 11

The Second Time Around

The program office re-announced the position. The new announcement contained significantly lessened job requirements. Would Dan be their man? As soon as the job was approved for a second time and posted, Kapitski received an email from USAJOBS indicating that the position that she had previously applied for had been re-.

Based on inter-office discussions, it now appeared that although they wanted to offer Bill the position, they were really going to play fair and square. Kaspitski consulted with her mentor again. Although she was coerced into declining further consideration the last time, maybe the rumors were untrue? So Kapitski decided to submit an application for the new announcement.

By the time the second announcement closed several other unsavory actions had taken place within the program office. This time a different member of management served as the hiring official. Shortly after receipt of the second list, the hiring official determined that interviews would be held with the highest qualified candidates.

Over the years, interoffice discussion revealed that the program office had attained a "bully" reputation of allegedly conducting shady personnel practices. These practices were apparently well within the shades of grey and difficult to prove if employees filed grievances or sought other remedies. It was widely known that most applicants rarely took them to task due to fear of retaliation.

As the process continued, interviews were scheduled. Kapitski was interviewed telephonically.

In spite of the varied responsibilities associated with the director position, the interview consisted of only three (3) questions. The questions were presented while the interviewing official was driving as Kapitski could hear horns and even sirens as the questions were being asked.

The interviewer had apparently called Kapitski while driving as she could clearly hear traffic sounds as the three questions were presented. In between sounds of traffic, sirens, and so forth, Kapitski provided thorough responses to each of the questions. After approximately 5-7 minutes, the interview was over.

*****

How would you describe an interview environment?

How would you describe the environment for Kapitski's second interview?

What do you think happened next?

Chapter 12

The Second Offer

Shortly after the interviews concluded, the hiring official submitted the package to HC requesting that an expedited tentative offer of employment be made to Bill. HC presented the tentative offer to Bill telephonically with a follow-up tentative letter offer via electronic mail. Bill was so eager that he accepted the offer during the initial call.

This hiring official notified Kapitski hat she was not selected for the position. He told her that she was the second best, but that Bill was the man! Just as soon as the offer was accepted, program officials announced that Bill would be coming on board.

*****

What are your thoughts now?

Chapter 13

The New Director

Bill reported for duty. It was soon apparent that Bill was "the man." Although the new director's expertise aligned with some programs, he would use his ear to program officials and his associated political clout to launch and contagiously dispatch his agenda.

Almost immediately, he began to harass Kapitski and a few other program managers in an ever so subtle manner - keeping consistent with the shades of gray and boldly misinterpreting the organization's long-standing policies on an "at will" basis.

It soon became clear that although Bill was

"the man," he initially display very few relationship building or team building skills using a dictatorial approach to manage senior staffers who for years had been self-managers or who had previously served as managers and supervisors themselves.

The closed door discussions continued as the organization prepared itself for the days ahead.

****

- **Do you see a shenanigan in action?**
- **What are Kapitski's options?**
- **What are the program managers' options?**
- **What happened within this program office?**
- **What happened within this organization?**

This case was based on true facts and circumstances involving a situation that occurred within a large federal organization. The names were changed to protect the privacy and identify of the individuals involved.

www.ShenanigansCaseStudies.com

About the Author

LTC (Ret) Dukes has written several case studies. Volume I is the first study published in this venue. She has a passion for excellence in leadership, management, communication, and service.

She has over twenty years of supervisory experience with the Department of Defense. She held four command positions in the United States Army including battalion command. Her leadership skills were identified early on as she commanded a company grade (Captain) command as a first lieutenant. She has managed large, geographically dispersed organizations consisting of both military and civilian personnel responsible for services and support to communities of over 18,000 personnel. In addition to her military successes, she attained much recognition during the nearly ten years of experience gained while managing organizations that consisted of only federal civilian personnel. She has experience in leading organizations through change to eliminate redundancy and create greater operational efficiencies. She also led an organization through a 40% downsizing effort, that offered many voluntary separation incentives and eventually landed in three iterations of a reduction-in-force required to achieve the targeted personnel strength.

She also has extensive experience in procurement and acquisition management, human capital management, supply chain management, government contracting, and workforce development. LTC (Ret) Dukes has demonstrated a unique ability to lead initiatives to reduce redundancy and eliminate duplicative processes within organizations.

She has held positions ranging from a Contracting Officer (unlimited warrant) to a Director of Contracts with responsibility for multi-million dollar contracts and billion-dollar contract administration portfolios. She has the ability to leverage private sector knowledge with public sector operations. She has successfully facilitated open dialogue between a broad spectrum of stakeholders and interested parties including the private sector, program managers, and procurement operations.

As a Human Capital Director, she led a team that provided specialized talent management and human resource support to a top-notch group of Army professionals. She also managed a human capital operation responsible for providing support to 3000 personnel. She has provided human capital subject management expertise to both the public and private sector. As a participant in a government to industry program at a Fortune 500 company, she worked extensively with supply chain management and world-wide purchasing initiatives resulting in significant savings.

LTC (Ret) Dukes' exemplary track record includes the exceptional ability to lead and manage in a diverse environment. She has managed organizations of professionals with competing interests and diverse technical and professional skills. She has also successfully worked with diverse individuals and led organizations comprised of individuals of various socioeconomic, political, ethnic, religious, racial and challenged backgrounds. She is a coalition builder, team builder, and a consensus builder, that challenges and motivates others to achieve the common goal.

As an adjunct faculty, she has taught both graduate and undergraduate courses in colleges and universities. She is frequently sought for advice stemming from her roles as a board member, consultant, motivational speaker, and workshop leader. She especially enjoys building the foundations necessary for a good work-life balance that contribute directly to increased productivity within the workplace.

LTC(Ret) Dukes is committed to creating opportunities for organizational, academic, and individual excellence. She believes that human capital is an organization's most important resource. She actively enjoys mentoring others to help promote knowledge sharing and multi-generational skills transfers. LTC (Ret) Dukes is an advocate of facilitating collaborative partnerships to create win-win opportunities.

She entered military service as a private. Her efforts during ROTC yielded Distinguished Military Graduate status; whereby, she entered the Regular Army as a second lieutenant. In uniform she received many honors, awards, and decorations. Her untiring efforts resulted in her being selected for promotion below-the-zone to the rank of Major (top 5% of her year group/class). She was promoted through the ranks and honorably retired as a Lieutenant Colonel. She was selected for residence attendance at the U.S. Army Senior Service College. LTC(Ret) Dukes is an alumni of Eastern Kentucky University, Golden Gate University, and the United States Army Command and General Staff College.

She is actively involved in her community with youth activities. She is also an advocate for the gifted and talented. She developed curriculums for youth confidence building, etiquette and financial literacy. The classes are often delivered through community outreach programs.

www.ShenanigansCaseStudies.com